BIG JIM AND THE WHITE-LEGGED MOOSE

Jim Arnosky

Lothrop, Lee & Shepard Books  N

NEW YORK

Big Jim's a wildlife artist.

It's his job each day to go

Outdoors to sketch the birds and beasts

Where they live and grow.

He's seen and drawn the wildcat
That screams from granite ledge,
And he knows where bears have clawed up
All the trees on Big Beech Ridge.

He's painted deer in every season
And sketched the autumn goose.
But he wasn't working one fall day
When he saw his biggest moose.

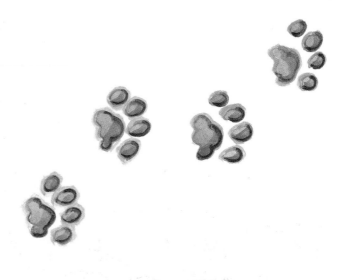

In our northern forest

A king of moose resides.

His crown is solid antler,

His robe a thick moose hide.

But his most distinctive feature,

What makes him unique,

Is the color of his legs—

All four pure white, down to his feet.

Jim was driving home from fishing
In a favorite forest lake,
When he came upon the giant moose
Standing squarely in his way.

He was nine feet tall from head to hoof.
His antlers spanned the road.
Trim and lean and bull moose mean,
All muscle, hair, and bone.

In our northern forest

A king of moose resides.

His crown is solid antler,

His robe a thick moose hide.

Jim saw him on the blacktop.

He posed regal and cool.

But Jim didn't have a pencil

For to draw the white-legged bull.

That sighting of the white-legged moose
Stuck in Big Jim's mind.
So next day he went back to the spot
The big bull's tracks to find.

An expert tracker, Big Jim was.
He soon was on the trail.
And all morning long he followed tracks
Over hill and vale.

The massive hoofprints led the way,

Getting fresher with each mile.

Jim felt his quarry wasn't far

And cracked a knowing smile.

He sharpened up his pencil,

And opened his sketchbook.

This time he wouldn't miss the chance

To sketch the white-legged bull.

Then from a stand of alders
Came a grunting, snorting sound.
And the bull moose stepped out wide-eyed mad,
At being followed all around.

Big Jim dropped his art supplies
And climbed a nearby birch.
With the bull below, Jim prayed,
As if he were in church.

But the bull moose didn't charge at all.
In answer to Jim's prayer,
It began to nibble sweet birch leaves,
As if Jim weren't there.

From his perch, Big Jim enjoyed
A view few artists see.
And once again, he wished he had his tools
To immortalize the scene.

In our northern forest

A king of moose resides.

His crown is solid antler,

His robe a thick moose hide.

Jim watched him feeding peaceably

Until he ate his full.

But Jim didn't have a pencil

For to draw the white-legged bull.

No, he didn't have a pencil

For to draw the white-legged bull.

In the autumn of 1987, I encountered the largest moose I have ever seen. It happened in much the same way described in this book. The moose was a bull with enormous antlers and distinctive white legs. After following his tracks on and off for many days, I finally saw the white-legged bull a second time. But unlike the Big Jim in my story, who was chased up a tree, I was able to stay hidden to quietly observe and actually make sketches of the great moose from life.

Ten years later, that experience inspired the humorous song "Big Jim and the White-Legged Moose." It's a good example of how sometimes even the tallest tale can have at its heart an actual event.

—Jim Arnosky

Ramtails, 1999

To Joyce and Bobby, Mischa and Max

Acrylics were used for the full-color illustrations.
The text type is 18-point Newtext Regular.

Published by Lothrop, Lee & Shepard Books
an imprint of Morrow Junior Books
a division of William Morrow and Company, Inc.
1350 Avenue of the Americas, New York, NY 10019
www.williammorrow.com

Printed in Hong Kong by South China Printing Company (1988) Ltd.

1 3 5 7 9 10 8 6 4 2

Library of Congress Cataloging-in-Publication Data
Arnosky, Jim.
Big Jim and the white-legged moose / Jim Arnosky.
p. cm.
Summary: A song about the time Big Jim had pencil and
sketchbook in hand while following the trail of a huge bull moose but
dropped his art supplies when he climbed a tree for safety.
ISBN 0-688-10864-4 (trade)—ISBN 0-688-10865-2 (library)
1. Children's songs—Texts. [1. Moose—Songs and music. 2. Songs.] I. Title.
PZ8.3.A648Bi 1999 782.42164'0268—dc21 [E] 98-21309 CIP AC

Chorus:

In our north-ern for-est A king of moose re-

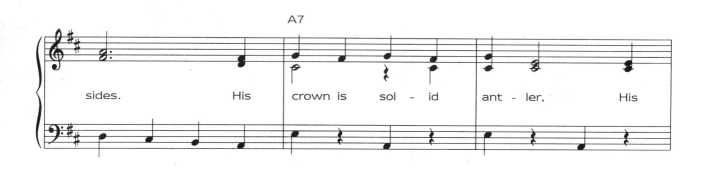

sides. His crown is sol-id ant-ler, His

robe a thick moose hide. But his most dis-tinc-tive

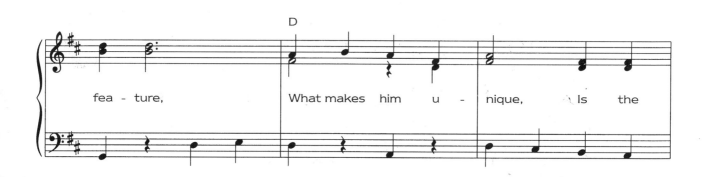

fea-ture, What makes him u-nique, Is the